Balboa Press
A Division of Hay House
1663 Liberty Drive
Bloomington, IN 47403
www.balboapress.com
844-682-1282

ISBN: 979-8-7652-4527-9 (hc)
ISBN: 979-8-7652-4484-5 (sc)
ISBN: 979-8-7652-4485-2 (e)

Library of Congress Control Number: 2023916159

Print information available on the last page.

Balboa Press rev. date: 10/17/2023

BALBOA.PRESS
A DIVISION OF HAY HOUSE

About the Author

Douglas Macauley lives in Germantown, Maryland. He is a dedicated father with children spanning two generations—a fourteen-year-old daughter and a thirty-four-year-old son. With degrees in electrical engineering and computer science, Douglas builds on his three decades as an electrical engineer in his work as a children's book author, mindfulness practitioner, life coach, and intuitive energy healer. Douglas is the author of *I Am a Feeling Body: Body Awareness and Mindfulness for Children* and *I Am Grounded: A Path to Stability and Feeling Safe*—part of a children's book series that teaches body awareness and mindfulness.

I Am Centered

Finding Your Point of Presence

By Douglas Macauley

Illustrated by Ariane Elsammak

About the Book

Expanding on *I Am a Feeling Body: Body Awareness and Mindfulness for Children* and focused on centering as the second essential tenet for finding your point of presence, *I Am Centered* is an empowering book about a boy and his two loving cats who explore the stillness that resides within themselves. They become curious and conscious of their bodies from this centered point of presence while finding the physical balance that reflects this inner awareness. Life becomes more enjoyable as they navigate both movement and stillness while staying grounded. Their lives become lighter and filled with love for one another as they feel gratitude for the fact that life is a gift to embrace.

For my dear children,
Mark and Madelyn:

Unconditional love and family are the keystones that hold us
all together. I am deeply grateful for having you in my life.

And in memory of and with deep gratitude for
my sweet and loving cats, Licorice and Taffi,
who always embodied unconditional love.

Note to Parents

Centering is the second of four essential tenets in creating a solid foundation to instill ongoing peace, harmony, happiness, and well-being in our lives. As described in my first book, *I Am a Feeling Body: Body Awareness and Mindfulness for Children*, these tenets include grounding, centering, breathing, and feeling as they relate directly to the awareness of and connection with the body. My second book, *I Am Grounded: A Path to Stability and Feeling Safe*, focuses on grounding as foundational for the body to feel connected with all that is; in turn it helps create a solid mind-body connection. *I Am Centered: Finding Your Point of Presence* expands on this body awareness by focusing on our inner stillness, which is critical for feeling freedom to navigate life with ease and grace.

When we connect with our inner stillness by finding our center, we begin to live more balanced lives. Our minds begin to relax into a state of equilibrium, and we allow our bodies to be guided by our heart. We can anchor our awareness in the wisdom of our hearts as our eternal center of gravity and in our anatomical physical center of gravity, which is located slightly below our navel. Integrating these two points of presence will allow us to stay balanced in all we do.

As we develop more bodily awareness, we begin to expand our continued sense of balance. Centering creates balance that allows us to navigate through life with ease, feeling lighter as we go while trusting the flow. We can relax into a deeper state of clarity and know that our bodily intelligence guides us in all we do. Along with being grounded, these two tenets form a very strong foundation within us to use. However, life occasionally creates challenges that cause us to lose ground and knock us off center. But we can more easily return to our center and reclaim our grounded state each and every time by returning to the feeling. Setting the intent and remembering the feeling will allow us to return to center and remain grounded. It is best to practice this on a regular basis so that we can return faster.

The feeling is similar to riding a bike; when we are centered, we can glide with ease and lightness while feeling free as the wind. Our nervous system and body become more relaxed, and activities require much less effort, allowing us to enjoy life.

When we create space each morning to engage ourselves in these steps, we produce profound results. We may also set the intention of having fun while creating a much stronger mind—body connection each and every day to start us on our way. It may take as little as ten minutes.

Although this book is intended primarily for children, it is valuable for any age group. When you absorb the initial meanings in the poems cognitively and somatically as one, the benefit grows exponentially. I hope that children will deepen their awareness and begin to associate feelings when seeing the illustrations, as these will become somatic bookmarks for returning them to a centered and grounded state of being.

When you lead your children through the exercises, allow them to discover the fun themselves so they will create their own personal experiences. There are no right or wrong ways to do this. Your children will find their way by using their bodies to guide them. Trust and allow. Amazing things will happen.

Relax your mind and feel your heart.
This is the foundational place to start.

"Be gentle with yourself."

Settle into your body and quiet your thoughts.
Your heart whispers kind words typically not taught.

"You are loved."

As we become deeply familiar with our body parts,
We begin to find center and stillness within our hearts.

Guided by feeling to our unique place of truth,
We relax and feel calm in the magic of youth.

Centering creates balance to ride through life with ease.
Peace flows through our body like a warm, flowing breeze.

Our whole body feels relaxed, not guarded or tense.
Deep clarity arrives as we feel and we sense.

Imagine yourself riding a bike—
Feeling centered, balanced, and
grounded alike.

The breeze flows through you, around you, above and below.
Your centered body feels light, with a triumphant glow.

This is the place where you are truly free
To explore life, feel happiness, and simply just be.
Anchor this feeling so deeply within you.

Believe it and know it, as this is
what's true.

Access this feeling each and every day.
This is your foundation as you go out to play.

When you're riding a bike,
playing baseball, or walking,

Stay centered every step, as you
may just be talking.

Practice and explore this all the time.
Find it to be easy as a soft, flowing rhyme.

Effortless, flowing as your heart and mind agree.
Wow! Your whole body lights up from sea to shining sea.

As you step off your bike feeling light as a breeze,
Remember to stay grounded as you see all the trees.

Grounded and centered are your best friends for sure.
They are the path to solidity, knowing you are safe and secure.

Heart centered and lightness help you take each step ahead.
Others' kindness and love will show up and spread.

Like water flowing, expanding, and easily finding its way,
Trust life the same as you navigate each day.

Take a moment to be grateful and honor yourself.
You are so amazing; you are life itself.

You now have some fun tools to steer you to reenter.
Focus on your heart to stay in your magic center.

Printed in the United States
by Baker & Taylor Publisher Services